P9-DMJ-077

contents

introduction

The magic of paperfolding

Have you ever seen someone take a sheet of ordinary paper and within a few moments turn it into a representation of a familiar subject, such as an animal, a bird or a human figure? Have you ever wished that you could emulate such a feat of simple yet magical dexterity? Origami, unlike any other art or craft, is unique in that it uses ordinary paper as its basic material. There's no need for any other materials or equipment such as scissors and glue; indeed, all you will require to make even the most complicated design are several sheets of paper and a smooth folding surface. Along with a little patience, neatness and accuracy as you work, and armed with a copy of this book, you will soon be skilfully proficient in producing a whole range of interesting paper models, from colourful flowers to delicate swans and pretty butterflies.

BELOW This two-tone valentine's heart, pierced by an arrow, has been cleverly folded from a single, uncut piece of paper.

This volume begins with traditional folds dating back centuries, and introduces simple designs, such as the Cup and the Crane, one of the most popular designs of ancient Japan. It proceeds to the wonderful Masu Box, which includes a majestic climax to the folding sequence, and typifies the elegant beauty of origami. The remaining projects are a selection from modern-day designers, and include the simple yet ingenious Nun, the similarly stylized Scottie Dog, the author's reworking of the well-known Swan, and Edwin Corrie's brilliant Rabbit fold, where the reverse colour of the paper cleverly forms the cotton tail.

What is origami?

Origami is the Japanese art of paperfolding. The name is derived from "ori" meaning to fold and "gami" meaning paper. Dictionaries often describe the art of origami as the making of simple forms such as birds from folded paper, and from this brief description or from childhood memories, you may be forgiven for thinking that origami is limited to paper aeroplanes and waterbombs. However, the last 30–40 years have seen great developments in the art of origami, so that it is now possible to represent almost anything in folded paper.

Modern design

In recent years there has been an enormous leap in the development of ideas and techniques. These are evident in the realization of three-dimensional constructions, pieces of origami that are made from more than a single sheet of paper, and others that use unusual shapes of paper, such as pentagons and hexagons. While the simplest and most elegant forms of origami are often the most pleasing to make, many modern designers are developing the art of paperfolding and producing exciting designs using a wide variety of papers and materials. Pat Crawford used paper that has two different sides with contrasting colours to great effect in her Valentine, a red heart pierced by a silver arrow, which is folded from a single uncut sheet of paper.

LEFT The Crane is a traditional design that many children learn to fold.

An American, Jeremy Shafer, designed a set of working Nail Clippers, which he made using very fine Japanese foil paper. He later developed a version made out of similarly fine metal sheeting.

Creating new pieces of origami is often a complex procedure, with the designer trying to implement an idea while taking account of the restrictions imposed by the medium. Most enthusiasts believe that origami is only produced from folding uncut paper. Indeed, purists will frown upon the mere mention of the words "cut" or "stick", and are unlikely to agree that the odd slit here and there to help make a fold possible is true origami. Such a cultured discipline however inspires those taking up the art to think and rethink their design objectives, and promotes much sharing of ideas as well as providing individuals with an intellectual challenge. Whatever your view, the most important thing is to enjoy origami for the beautiful and creative art form it most surely is.

Materials

The paper you choose for each design is very important. Paper is one of the most common materials, it is available in a range of thicknesses and textures, and each type varies in its ability to hold creases. Suggestions have been given for a suitable paper to use for each project, but your own experiments and initiative will be a factor as you practise folding different models. You may find that you need to fold two or three practice models using different types of paper before deciding on the paper that you feel is best for the final version. Shop around and discover the wealth of papers that are available. Look out for different textures and colours to add to your collection. Even if you have no immediate use for it – it could be just what you need for a project that turns up later.

HOW TO USE THIS BOOK

Start at the beginning, and give yourself time to become familiar with all you need to know in preparation for model making. Study the following sections on paper, techniques and base folds. When you have learned these procedures thoroughly, you can confidently start making the designs in this book to a standard that will please and satisfy you. Each chapter begins with simple projects that progress towards more challenging designs. While you are folding, consider what is commonly known as the "look ahead rule": when you are following individual illustrations, look at least two or three steps ahead, to check how things should turn out. You may even turn to the final steps, so that you can see the completed project. This will encourage you enormously.
Do not allow yourself to become discouraged. Persevere, try and try again, take your time, and enjoy your paperfolding.

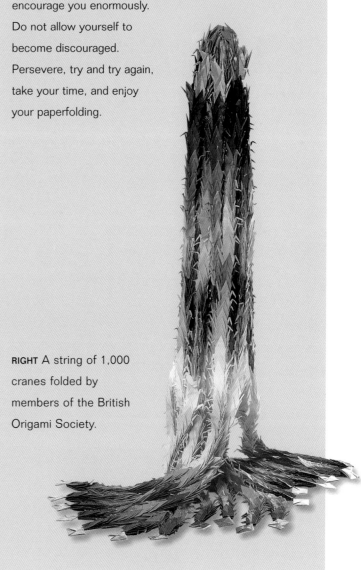

RIGHT A string of 1,000 cranes folded by members of the British Origami Society.

the art of
origami

the art of
origami

an illustrated guide to Japanese paperfolding,
with over 30 classic designs

rick beech

southwater

To David Connor, with grateful thanks:
Everyone remembers a wonderful teacher.

This edition is published by Southwater

Southwater is an imprint of Anness Publishing Limited
Hermes House, 88–89 Blackfriars Road, London SE1 8HA
tel. 020 7401 2077; fax 020 7633 9499;
www.southwaterbooks.com; info@anness.com

© Anness Publishing Limited 2003

UK agent: The Manning Partnership Ltd
tel. 01225 478 444; fax 01225 478 440
sales@manning-partnership.co.uk

UK distributor: Grantham Book Services Ltd
tel. 01476 541 080; fax 01476 541 061
orders@gbs.tbs-ltd.co.uk

North American agent/distributor: National Book Network
tel. 301 459 3366; fax 301 429 5746
www.nbnbooks.com

Australian agent/distributor: Pan Macmillan Australia
tel. 1300 135 113; fax 1300 135 103
customer.service@macmillan.com.au

All rights reserved. No part of this publication may be reproduced,
stored in a retrieval system, or transmitted in any way or by any
means, electronic, mechanical, photocopying, recording or otherwise,
without the prior written permission of the copyright holder.

A CIP catalogue record for this book is available from the
British Library.

Publisher Joanna Lorenz
Managing Editor Linda Fraser
Project Editor Mary Pickles
Photography John Freeman
Design Penny Dawes
Jacket Design Balley Design
Production Controller Darren Price

Previously published as part of a larger volume, *Origami*

10 9 8 7 6 5 4 3 2 1

The author and publishers would like to thank the origamists who
contributed their designs to this book:
Angela Baldo p10; Paul Bascetta pp 50–53; Ruthanne Bessman
p12; Alfred Bestall pp66–67; Jeff Beynon p14; David Brill
pp14–15, 50–53; Adolfo Cerceda pp88–95; Edwin Corrie
pp72–75; Nobuyoshi Enomoto pp82–87; Alfredo Giunta p11;
Alice Gray pp46–47, 61–63; Andrew Hans p10; Robert
Harbin p41; Paul Jackson pp56–57, 61–63; Eric Joisel p13;
Kunihiko Kasahara pp54–55, 76–81; Toshikazu Kawasaki p11;
Robert Lang p12; David Mitchell p13; Robert Neale p60;
Masamichi Noma pp68–71; Chris Palmer p14; Toshie Takahama
pp76–81; Florence Temko pp64–65; Akira Yoshizawa p11

A Gallery of Origami Masterpieces

The inspirational paper masterpieces created by the
world's finest origamists are truly stunning.
It takes years of practice to develop the dexterity
and patience to fold pieces such as David Brill's
magnificent animals or Alfredo Giunta's miniature
creations, and unarguable natural artistic skill
to be able to create such interesting
and innovative designs.

gallery

The following pages show a range of designs by origami masters from all corners of the world, displaying a variety of materials and folding techniques. Each one a masterpiece.

$5 Intersecting Tetrahedra

BELOW The original model, which measures 15cm x 15cm (6in x 6in), was designed by Tom Hull and folded from ordinary paper. Fellow American Andrew Hans decided to see whether the same model could be folded out of American dollar bills (often the proportions of the paper can make a difference, of course).

Andrew Hans, 1999

Shell

LEFT Many folders enjoy the challenge of modifying an original design, either by themselves or by another creator. Here, American enthusiast Angela Baldo has produced a variation on a classic seashell design by Toshikazu Kawasaki, the principle being the same, that of a spiral twist to complete the lock. The use of a topographical map from a US Geographical survey is very striking.

Angela Baldo, 1999

Bees and Honeycomb

RIGHT Miniature models belong to certain specialists, one of whom is Italian folder Alfredo Giunta, who has designed this multi-model tiny masterpiece; the bees incidentally are about 3.5 cm (1⅜in) long! Many of Alfredo's designs are folded from tissue foil, i.e. tissue paper that is back-coated on to either aluminium or paper-backed foil wrapping.

Alfredo Giunta, 1996

Wolf and Cubs

LEFT The recognized master of origami is the Japanese expert Akira Yoshizawa, who has given the world many wonderful designs. Mr Yoshizawa continues to produce work of an amazing high standard, exhibiting throughout the world. He is a fine exponent of wet folding, and has developed his own special paper. This wolf and cubs is an example of his mastery.

Akira Yoshizawa, 1995

Rose and Leaves

RIGHT Japanese folder Toshikazu Kawasaki has designed many variations on an original rose model created several years ago, which has become a classic. This example, which is 7cm (2¾in) in length, uses a typically clever collapsing twist, which sees the model formed into a tube, before the final curling of the petals produces the beautiful rose.

Toshikazu Kawasaki, 1993

Greetings Cards

LEFT Often the presentation of origami, however simple, is the most important part of enjoying your art, and the making of greetings cards is something that many folders consider. Award-winning card maker Ruthanne Bessman (US) uses simple and traditional folds to produce elegant results.

Ruthanne Bessman, 1999

Scorpion and Cicada

ABOVE AND BELOW LEFT American Robert Lang creates some of the most technically impressive models, such as a one-piece working cuckoo clock. Robert wet folds the majority of his models, like the two wonderful creatures illustrated here, which are 13–15cm (5–6 in) in length.

Robert Lang, 1987

Mask

RIGHT French designer Eric Joisel recently devised his own particular style of producing masks, using different kinds of paper, in a seemingly free style of sculpture. Those that argue as to whether origami is an art form or not might be swayed to the former opinion by Eric's beautiful creations. He has sold many of his models to enthusiastic buyers around the world.

Eric Joisel, 1999

Paper Crystals

ABOVE LEFT, ABOVE AND RIGHT Taken from a book of the same name, Paper Crystals are modular constructions made of simple units, designed by Englishman David Mitchell. David has written several books on modular folding and paper puzzles, and continues to develop new ideas within this particular type of origami.

David Mitchell, 1989 and 1995

Boxes

LEFT Using intricate crease patterns and tessellations, American Chris Palmer's boxes and flowers are collapsed into a certain shape, known as a "tato", then completely unfolded, new creases added, and collapsed once more in varying stages to give beautiful symmetry and form. The smallest box is 3cm squared (1¼in) and the largest is 10 cm squared (4in).

Chris Palmer, 1996

Rhinoceros, Elephant and Horse

RIGHT ABOVE AND BELOW Quite the most prolific and talented British folder has to be David Brill, who has fashioned over the years some incredible masterpieces, like this horse, which is 16cm (6¼in) long, and created from a triangular sheet of paper! It is also wet folded, like so many of David's animal designs, including this elephant and rhinoceros.

David Brill, mid 1970s

Spring into Action

LEFT This action toy was designed by Welsh folder Jeff Beynon in the early nineties. There are lots of pre-creases made before the twist-collapse is performed, and it is not an easy design to reproduce accurately. One holds the model, which is 2.5cm (1in) when flat, by the centre wheel, and squeezes gently, causing the spring action and the model to extend to 17.5cm (6¾in).

Jeff Beynon, 1991

Paper, Techniques & Base Folds

Before you begin folding the models that appear in

this book, it is essential that you first become

familiar with the properties of certain papers and

recognize the importance of folding accurately.

You will also need to acquire a firm grasp of simple

procedures and some more complex moves, such as

inside reverse folds, rabbit ears and sinks.

Once committed to memory, these specialized

techniques will give you the skills you need to

produce absolutely anything, at any level,

in origami.

paper

Although most origami models can be folded from almost any type of paper, there are certain designs that beg for the use of specialist material, whether purely for aesthetic beauty, or because of the weight and thickness of the chosen medium. A wide variety of interesting and unusual papers can now be purchased from gift shops, stationers and specialist shops alike, or even found around the home. Enjoy experimenting with different types of paper.

Duo paper

Paper with a different colour on the reverse side is a great asset to origami enthusiasts, as it helps provide areas of alternate colour to finished models. Available in pre-cut specialist packs, you can now find such paper in standard-size packs and even in rolls. Look out for paper that is described as 'fadeless duo' and is sold as art material.

Specialist origami paper

Pre-cut packs of multi-coloured origami paper, available in a wide variety of sizes, colours and patterns, are not that easy to find locally. Thankfully, origami societies around the world have an excellent mailing service supplying different types and sizes of paper, as do a number of specialist suppliers. This kind of paper is fairly flimsy, yet will crease well, so it is ideal for practising your models, although you may prefer to use a different material once you have mastered a particular design.

Textured paper

As well as patterned paper, there are also many different kinds of paper available that have a texture to the surface. This proves particularly useful when folding animals and other living creatures, as it enhances the realism of the subject. Such papers as elephant hide, Ingres and watercolour can also be ideal wet folding mediums.

Metallic, foil, opaque & shiny papers

These are some of the more difficult materials to work with, but if you persevere the results can look spectacular. Paper-backed foil is widely available, and this material has the property of being able to be curved and moulded. Care must be taken, however, as some foil papers, thin plastic materials and opaque paper can be quite difficult to crease well, and reversed creases can crack, whiten or even split.

Washi & other handmade paper

In specialist paper shops you can buy Japanese washi paper, which is a soft, fibred material. This and other handmade papers from around the world give lighter creases to your folding and a softer, less angular look to final models.

Patterned paper

Gift wrap can be wonderful paper to fold with, as it is often quite sturdy (medium weight) and nowadays there is so much choice around. Look out for musical manuscript, swirling watermark-patterned paper, wood grain appearance and abstract gold, black and silver colourings in gift shops and the larger department stores.

Materials from around the home

Before you go searching for special or expensive paper to fold with, remember that your home may be already a great source of folding material. Copy paper, napkins, spare wallpaper, index cards, bank notes (those foreign currencies saved from holiday expeditions), and even magazines or newspapers can be used to make interesting and practical origami models.

equipment and preparation

There are very few essential origami tools to purchase, or preparation techniques to learn. However, it is worth familiarizing yourself with tools you might need, many of which, such as scissors and rulers, are household items, and making sure that they are within reach before you begin folding.

spray adhesive

guillotine

self-heal cutting ma

pencil

metal ruler

craft knife

scissors

Equipment

Although plenty of origami models can be made with nothing more than a piece of paper and a pair of hands, there are a few pieces of equipment that are essential to a dedicated origamist. Spray adhesive is useful for sticking two sheets of different-coloured or textured paper together, but always follow the safety instructions. A guillotine is a worthwhile investment if you are practising origami on a regular basis. They come in a variety of sizes and a range of prices and have the advantage of cutting a very straight edge. A cutting knife is a very useful tool as its extremely sharp blade makes cutting through any thickness of paper simple. Always use a metal ruler when working with a craft knife and rest the paper on a self-healing cutting mat. This will not only protect the work surface, but will also prevent slipping and thus accidental cuts, as well as extending the life of the blade. A sturdy pair of paper scissors can often be just as effective as any other cutting tool, but make sure that you draw a faint, accurate pencil line on the paper before you start to cut.

Using a guillotine

Often you will require a specific size of paper, and a guillotine is a great help here, particularly as you can align your paper with the straight measured edge to ensure that you make a cut that is at right angles to the straight edge. It is possible to cut two or three sheets at a time, but you will get a cleaner cut if you only cut one sheet at a time.

1 Place one edge of the paper flush with the ruled edge of the guillotine.

2 Holding the paper in place with one hand, use your other hand to slide the cutting blade across it, making a clean accurate cut.

Spray mounting

Spray mounting two sheets of paper together, back to back, is a useful technique for thickening an existing outer paper for a certain project, or for providing a chosen combination of colours. Spray mounting foil paper to tissue paper yields a material that can be shaped and moulded, curved and sculptured more easily than conventional paper, while the tissue paper gives a more realistic look to living creatures.

1 Protect your worksurface with newspaper. Select two sheets of paper, and lay one face down on your spraying surface. Using spray adhesive, spray a fine mist evenly across the paper.

2 Carefully place the reverse side of the second sheet (the side you do not wish to be visible) on top of the upturned sticky first sheet. The second sheet should ideally be slightly smaller than the first, so that a thin border will appear around the edges of this second sheet.

3 Carefully smooth out any wrinkles or creases in the back-coated layers by running your hand over the upper surface, pressing firmly as you go.

4 With a craft knife and ruler, or with a guillotine, trim off the excess paper around the edges.

SAFETY

As with all aerosols, it is important to read the instructions on the spray adhesive can and follow them closely. If possible, use the spray outside and wear a mask. Otherwise, make sure that you are in a well-ventilated area and that you have protected the surfaces around you. Newspaper and cardboard offer cheap and effective protection.

techniques and tips

Although you are probably keen to get started on the projects, read this section first so that you understand the standard techniques and basic procedures before you make a model. Learning how to fold your paper correctly, and familiarizing yourself with the photograph step instructions are key stages to successful models. The more you practise folding the basic techniques the more you will enjoy making origami.

How to fold

The first golden rule is to have something smooth and flat to use as your folding surface, preferably of a larger area than the sheet of paper that you are going to fold. The second is to make all the creases in the paper, by folding in a direction away from you, taking the edge or corner nearest to you and folding bottom to top. This is simply to make the folding easier, and to give you more control over the paper than if you tried to bring the upper edge or corner towards you or by folding side to side.

Wherever possible, the photographs will follow a natural folding sequence so that you will not need to alter the position or orientation of the paper in order to fold away from you. Always make firm, sharp creases. The neater and sharper you make the creases, the better the finished model will appear. Do not hurry to finish the model. Relax, take care and enjoy what you are folding. Do not be discouraged if your first attempt ends in disappointment, because you have not been able to complete the model. If it is not as well folded as the illustration suggests, just try again.

Ways to fold

Technically, there are only two actual ways to fold: either a valley fold, where a corner, edge or flap will remain to the front and in sight; or a mountain fold, taking a portion of the paper behind the rest of the model and out of sight. All other folds are variations of the valley and mountain folds.

Valley fold

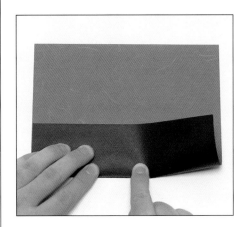

1 Fold the lower edge of the paper upward, to an arbitrary point. Hold the fold in place with one hand, and smooth out the crease with the other hand.

2 This is a valley (or forward) fold.

Mountain fold

1 With fingers and thumbs at the ends of the crease you intend to make, fold the paper behind, pinching in the fold. Here, the fold is made to a corner.

2 Smooth out the crease. This is a mountain (or backward) fold.

Pre-crease

Often you will fold and unfold the paper in order to leave a crease which will act as a guideline for a later definite fold. This is called a pre-crease.

Pinch crease

1 Sometimes when you are making a crease, you do not actually want to crease through every layer of paper, or even all the way across the paper, but wish to make a tiny mark or short crease line to act as a guide for a later definite fold. To do this, simply apply pressure to a part of the fold.

2 Unfold, leaving a small crease mark as your guide.

Dividing into thirds

Often you will need to be able to fold the paper accurately into three equal parts or thirds. This procedure is a little experimental, so take your time and fold carefully.

1 Using a rectangular sheet of paper, and with the shorter sides horizontal, fold the lower edge upward, to a point which you judge to be one-third of the way down from the upper edge. Make a very soft crease.

2 Fold the upper edge down over the section of paper folded in step 1. Make a soft crease. Unfold the paper. If you have estimated the flap in step 1 correctly, you should now have three horizontal borders of equal depth. Each outer raw edge could then be folded inward, and would meet with one of the creases made in steps 1–2. If you are slightly out in your estimation, then try again, making the initial crease slightly higher or lower than before.

Pleat fold

This is the concertina effect produced when a flap is doubled back on itself.

1 Make two parallel valley folds in a sheet of paper. Turn the paper over so that these horizontal creases are now mountain creases.

2 Pinch the lower crease between fingers and thumb of each hand. Slide this crease and the paper beneath away from you, until you can lie it upon the upper crease. Flatten the model.

ABOVE The completed pleat fold.

Special moves

There are several special moves in origami, standard techniques that are used in countless models in one form or another. Once you have learned these basic routines you will always be able to adapt your skill and knowledge to whichever project you are tackling.

Inside reverse fold

This is one of the most common procedures, which occurs in two basic forms: tucking a flap inside the model or changing the angle of a point.

Tucking a flap inside

1 Fold a rectangular sheet of paper in half and rotate the paper 180° so that the fold you have just made now runs horizontally across the top.

2 Fold the vertical side at the right down so that it lies along the lower edge.

3 Unfold step 2.

4 By slightly opening out the fold made in step 1 you will see that the crease made in step 2 runs through both sides of the paper. One of the creases will appear as a valley fold, the other as a mountain fold. Both need to be mountain folds, so pinch the valley fold into a mountain fold.

5 Pushing inwards on the spine crease that originally ran along the upper edge of the right-hand portion of the paper, allow the triangular flap to be turned inside out, as it is pushed between the outer layers of the paper.

6 Allow the two outer corners to come back together as you flatten the paper.

ABOVE The completed inside reverse fold.

Folding a point

1 Fold a piece of paper into a Kite base (see p.30), then fold in half lengthways along the centre crease.

2 Make an arbitrary valley fold as shown, bringing the point downwards, and changing the angle of the point.

3 Unfold step 2.

4 Slightly open out the two lower sloping edges at the right, that run to the point, and see how the crease made in step 2 passes through both layers of the paper, front and back. Once again, make both creases forming the V shape mountain folds (change the direction of the valley fold to a mountain fold), as you begin to push down on the spine crease running along the upper right edge.

5 Allow the paper to turn inside out, as the spine crease of the point bends backwards on itself and is pushed down between the two outer layers.

ABOVE The completed inside reverse fold.

Outside reverse fold

This move is similar to the inside reverse fold, except that the layers of paper are wrapped around the outside in order to effect the angle change.

1 Prepare the point by folding a Kite base (see p.30), then fold this in half lengthways using the centre crease.

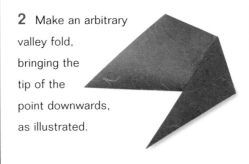

2 Make an arbitrary valley fold, bringing the tip of the point downwards, as illustrated.

3 Unfold step 2.

4 Open out the two upper edges leading to the tip of the point. As with the inside reverse fold, the crease made in step 2 now passes through both layers of paper, front and back.

5 Using the existing V shape of creases, turn the point outside on itself. The spine crease leading to the tip of the point is changed in direction from a valley fold to a mountain fold.

6 Allow the front and rear layers to come back together as you flatten the paper.

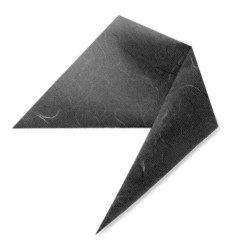

ABOVE The completed outside reverse fold.

Rabbit ear

This is where two adjacent edges are folded in simultaneously. As the two edges come together, they are squashed to form another point.

1 Fold a square of paper in half from corner to corner. Unfold.

2 Rotate the paper around so that the crease made in step 1 is now vertical to you, then fold the paper in half once more, corner to corner, making a second crease perpendicular to the first. Unfold.

3 Fold the lower left sloping edge upward to lie along the horizontal centre crease.

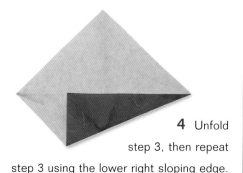

4 Unfold step 3, then repeat step 3 using the lower right sloping edge.

5 Unfold step 4. Simultaneously refold the lower sloping edges as folded in steps 3–4, to the centre crease.

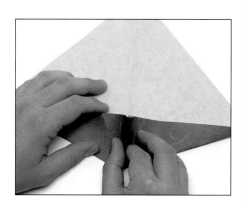

6 Squeeze the corner nearest to you to a point, using the vertical diagonal crease. The new point will project upwards at right angles to the rest of the model.

RIGHT The completed rabbit ear.

Squash fold

This is where a flap is squashed down into a new position.

1 Fold a square of paper in half diagonally, then in half again. Unfold the second stage and arrange so that the folded edge runs along the top. Raise the right-hand flap of the model upward on the vertical centre crease, so that it is at right angles to the folding surface.

2 Separate the two layers of the raised flap with one hand, and with your other hand squash the paper flat, bringing the spine crease of the raised flap down to lie along the vertical crease.

RIGHT The completed squash fold.

Crimp fold

This is a useful move for adding a 3D effect or sculptured look to models.

1 Fold a rectangular sheet of paper in half, bringing the shorter sides together. Rotate the paper around so that the shorter sides are now horizontal. Make an arbitrary valley fold in the paper, at about the halfway mark, but at an angle, so that the portion of paper that you are folding comes to rest offset to the left.

2 Fold the upper flap back downwards on itself, making another valley crease. At the right as you look, this crease begins at the same place as the crease made in step 1, so that when you pull the paper back downward, you do so as far as you can comfortably go.

3 Open out all the creases. You will now see that the two creases you made in steps 1–2 pass through both layers of the paper, front and back. Whether you want to make an inside or an outside crimp (see final pictures), you need to adopt the same principle as with the inside and outside reverse folds: on one side of the model the valley and mountain creases are in the opposite direction to the same creases on the other side of the paper. Opposite pairs of the same crease need to be either both valley folds, or mountain folds. You will, therefore, need to change the direction manually of both creases on one side of the paper.

4 Step 5 completed, seen from above, showing the principal crease from step 1 restored. Take hold of the paper with each hand, at opposite ends of this folded edge.

5 Holding the left side of the paper firmly in place, allow the right hand to bring the right portion of the paper downwards. The creases made in steps 1–2 will now allow the paper to flatten into the position shown. Both sides of the paper will appear identical. This is an outside crimp, where the crease furthest to the right is a mountain fold.

ABOVE The completed outside crimp fold.

ABOVE If the crease furthest to the right is a valley crease, then the result will be as shown. The completed inside crimp fold.

Swivel fold

Fairly lengthy preparation is needed in order to be able to illustrate and practise this origami move.

1 Fold the paper in half, corner to opposite corner, to pre-crease the diagonal. Unfold and arrange as a square. Fold the lower left corner and lower edge upward to lie along the diagonal crease line.

2 Fold the lower right corner directly upwards by an arbitrary amount.

3 Unfold step 2. Fold the left-hand edge across making a vertical crease perpendicular to the upper edge. This crease should meet with the crease made in step 2.

4 Unfold step 3.

5 Now, keeping the triangular flap folded in step 1 in place, refold the crease from step 2 in the underside layer only, which will cause the paper of the upper layer at the right-hand side to lift up, and not to lie flat.

6 The paper should naturally "crimp" across to the left, where the vertical valley crease in the upper layer of the paper pulls the excess material with it. The central area of paper then seems to "swivel" into place. Flatten the model. The completed swivel fold.

Sink fold

This move entails a closed point to be sunk inside the model. You may need to practise this move several times before you perfect it.

1 Prepare a Waterbomb base (see pp.32–3).

2 Fold the top corner down by an arbitrary amount.

3 Unfold step 2, then open the Waterbomb base out slightly, and look at the model from above.

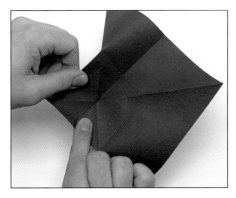

4 In the centre of the paper you will locate a small square, which was created by the crease made in step 2, passing through all the layers of the paper. Pinch-crease all these creases as mountain folds. Some are mountain folds already.

5 Pushing this central square inwards on existing creases, carefully collapse the Waterbomb base once again.

6 Flatten the paper, ensuring that there are two flaps to the left and two flaps to the right of the Waterbomb base. What was the central square has now become inverted into the model. The completed sink fold.

Wet folding

Making origami with damp paper allows you to mould and shape the model to a greater degree than you can with dry paper. Start off with a simple model that you have folded many times before, one without pointed corners and sharp creases. The larger the square you start with, the thicker the paper you can use.

1 To dampen the paper, use a damp sponge or absorbent cloth and carefully brush both sides of the paper until the sheet is uniformly damp. The key word is damp; not wet. Only experience can really tell you how damp the paper needs to be, but if it becomes shiny, allow it to dry slightly before proceeding.

2 Once a crease has been made, you can use the warmth of your fingers to partially dry out that area so it will retain its shape.

3 Continue to crease the paper while moulding the folds as required. Master-folder Robert Lang recommends using masking tape to help reinforce weak areas of the paper (such as where several creases meet). The tape can be removed when the paper is dry.

4 Since the aim of wet folding is "animation" of the fold, you should encourage three-dimensionality wherever possible and keep non-essential creases to a minimum. A consequence is that most of your folding will have to be performed in the air.

5 The feel and appearance of wet-folded origami is impossible to match in any other way.

base folds

Throughout ancient Japanese origami tradition, as well as by contemporary experimentation, certain basic folds, or bases, have evolved. These are standard and easily recognizable starting points from which hundreds of different models derive. It is worth committing these to memory along with the miscellaneous tips and techniques from the preceding pages. Allow them to become familiar, enjoy folding them, and try to understand the crease patterns and formations of each of them, as they will appear in so many wonderful designs. Almost anyone can do origami, as long as they take the utmost care in following the instructions. Do not assume anything, but look closely at each photograph and text caption, until you clearly understand what you are required to do. With time and practice, you will be able to fold many of the models in this book without reading the text.

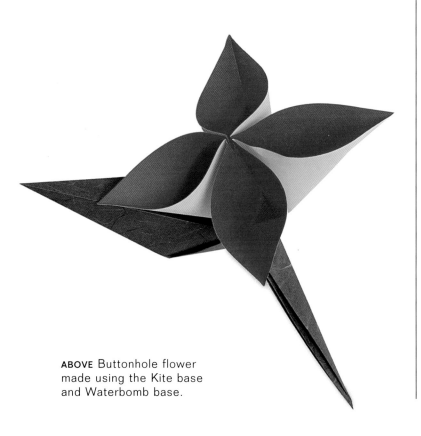

ABOVE Buttonhole flower made using the Kite base and Waterbomb base.

Kite base

1 Begin by folding a square of paper in half diagonally, bringing together two opposite corners. Unfold the paper and rotate it so that the crease you have just made is vertical to you, that is it runs from the upper corner to the lower corner, when the paper is arranged as a diamond, as shown.

2 Fold each of the lower sloping outer edges inward to lie along the vertical crease line made in step 1. The completed Kite base.

Blintz fold

Deriving from a Yiddish word of Ukrainian origin, a blintz is literally a thin pancake folded to contain a cheese or other filling. Because a blintz is folded with all the outer corners to the centre, the name was taken by Gershon Legman and other 1950s paperfolders to refer to the act of folding all the four corners of the square of paper to the centre. There are two principal methods to achieve this, both shown here. The second method is best when teaching origami to children and to the blind and partially-sighted, for it is far simpler to aim for a folded edge than to try to bring the four outer corners to a point within the area of paper.

method 1

1 Fold a square of paper in half diagonally, bringing together opposite corners. Unfold, rotate the paper so that the crease you have just made is now vertical to you (it runs from the upper corner to the lower corner), then fold in half again, bottom to top. This will add a pre-crease perpendicular to the first crease you made. Unfold once more.

2 Carefully fold each of the four outer corners in turn to the centre, that is where the two diagonal creases you made in step 1 intersect. There should be no overlap with any of the new corners formed, and all the raw edges should run evenly side by side to the centre. The completed Blintz fold.

method 2

1 Begin with the predominant colour face upwards. Arrange the paper on your folding surface so that it appears as a square, in other words, with horizontal and vertical sides. Fold the lower edge up to the upper edge, then rotate the paper 180° so that the fold you made in step 1 now runs horizontally along the upper edge.

2 Fold the lower outer corners, single layer only, upward, so that what were the vertical raw edges now lie along the upper horizontal edge.

3 Turn the paper over and repeat step 2 on this side of the paper.

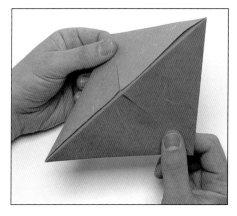

4 Take hold of the two independent corners at the right angle of the triangular form created in step 3, and pull apart.

5 Lay the paper flat on your folding surface, with the blintzed flaps on top. The completed Blinz fold.

Fish base

1 Begin by folding the Kite base.

2 Turn the paper over, keeping the sharper of the two points at either end of the diagonal fold at the bottom.

3 Fold the lower sharp point up to the top, folding the model in half.

4 Turn the paper over, keeping it arranged the same way.

5 At the lower half of the model, you have two independent flaps. Holding down the right-hand half of the model flat to your folding surface, take hold of the loose outer corner of the flap on the left side, and pull it towards you, allowing the pocket behind to open up. As you do this, carefully begin squashing the outer left-hand edge inward, lining up the new creases that you are making with both the upper corner and the corner you have just pulled down and repositioned.

6 Step 5 completed.

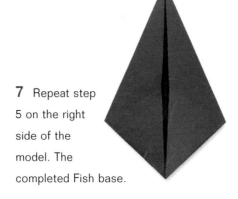

7 Repeat step 5 on the right side of the model. The completed Fish base.

Waterbomb base

1 Fold a square of paper in half, bringing opposite corners together. Unfold, then rotate the paper so that the first crease is vertical to you. Fold in half corner to corner once more, adding a pre-crease that is perpendicular to the first crease. Unfold once more.

2 Turn the paper over, and make a further pre-crease, folding the paper in half side to side, then unfold and turn back over to the original side. The diagonal creases will appear as valleys, while the remaining crease, which needs to be arranged horizontally across the paper, is a mountain.

3 With one finger, push down on the paper at the centre. The creases in the paper will flex gently, and the centre will show indications of becoming concave.

4 Take hold of the paper between fingers and thumbs of either hand along the vertical side edges, at a point just below the horizontal crease made in step 2.

5 Using the existing lower-diagonal creases, carefully bring the two sides in to meet, the sides flattening down to lie upon the central triangular area at the lower half of the paper.

6 Squash the upper layer of the paper flat, so that all the creases collapse into position, forming a pyramid. The completed Waterbomb base.

Preliminary base

1 Using a square of paper with the predominant colour face up, fold the paper in half, bringing opposite corners together. Unfold the paper then fold the paper in half again, bringing the remaining two corners together. Unfold again, and turn the paper over.

2 Now fold the paper in half side to side in both directions, each time folding the outer edges together and unfolding. The principle is the same as when folding the pre-creases in step 1.

3 Refold one of the creases made in step 2. Then take hold of the paper between fingers and thumbs of either hand, placed about halfway across each side of the paper, as shown.

4 In an upward circular motion, bring all your fingers and thumbs together simultaneously, causing all the four outer corners of the paper to meet at the top.

5 Flatten the model. This is achieved by swinging the large flap projecting upward down to one side, whilst swivelling the flap underneath the model across to the other side. There should now be two flaps pointing to the left, and two pointing to the right.

ABOVE The completed Preliminary base.

Bird base

1 Fold a Preliminary base, and begin by arranging the paper so that the open end, where the raw edges and corners meet, lies pointing toward you. Fold the lower sloping edges of the upper layer of the paper inward to lie along the vertical centre crease.

2 Fold the upper corner (the closed point) down over the flaps folded in step 1. Make a firm crease.

3 Unfold steps 1–2, so that you are back with the Preliminary base.

4 Using the crease made in step 2, lift up the single layer of paper at the lower corner, and raise it upward. The paper opens out, and this corner now comes to lie upon your folding surface.

5 Now allow the sides to be squashed inward to meet the vertical centre line. Steps 4–5 are often referred to as a petal fold.

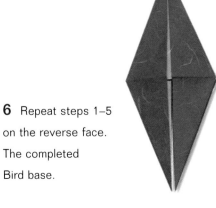

6 Repeat steps 1–5 on the reverse face. The completed Bird base.

Frog Base

1 Begin with a Preliminary base, and arrange so that the open end, where the raw edges and corners meet, lies pointing toward you.

2 Using the vertical centre crease as an axis by which all the large triangular flaps can be rotated, lift up one flap at the right, so that it projects outward at right angles to the rest of the model.

3 Separating the two layers of this flap, place one finger inside the pocket, and allow the paper to open and hollow out. With your other hand, squash the paper down, allowing the spine crease along the upper edge of this flap to come to rest along the centre line.

4 Step 3 completed.

5 You now have an upper section of paper resembling a kite shape. Using the vertical axis once again, fold the right half of this kite shape to the left.

6 You can now raise a second large flap from the right, and repeat steps 3–4. Repeat steps 3–4 in the same way with the remaining two large flaps, rotating the layers as you proceed.

7 With the squash folds from step 6 showing on the upper surface, fold the lower raw edges either side inward to lie along the vertical centre crease.

8 Unfold step 7.

9 We are now going to perform a petal fold similar to that of the Bird base. Carefully lift up the raw edge which cuts across the paper, connecting left and right outer corners of the model. Taking the single layer only, fold this edge upwards, making a valley crease horizontally across the paper, joining the upper extremes of the creases made in step 7. You will need to pinch this crease in manually. Allow the two outer edges to squash inward to the centre line.

10 Carefully manipulate the paper so that this petal fold lines up evenly with the vertical centre line, where the new point should rest.

11 Step 10 completed on one flap. Repeat steps 7–10 on the three similar faces, rotating the layers around the central vertical axis to accomplish this.

RIGHT The completed Frog base.

The Projects

Classic origami designs of ancient Chinese and

Japanese origin have been popular for centuries,

and here you will find traditional favourites such as

the crane, the dove and the sampan. There are also

models of other birds, animals, people and flowers

to make, many of them quite simple, and all of

them an excellent introduction to paperfolding.

crane

This is a traditional design that many Japanese children learn to fold. The crane is a symbol of peace and friendship; in Japan, multiple joined cranes are made in different combinations by preparing paper in which slits are cut, dividing the square into several smaller squares. The Hiroshima memorial is annually decorated with strings of a thousand brightly coloured cranes.

Crisp, brightly coloured paper is ideal for this design.

1 Begin by folding a Bird base. The two independent points should be facing toward you.

2 On the upper layer only, fold the two outer edges inward to lie along the vertical centre line.

3 Repeat step 2 on the reverse face.

4 Inside reverse fold both of the sharp points into the position shown.

5 Inside reverse fold the tip of one of the points to form the head.

6 Take hold of each of the wings and carefully pull them apart, allowing the central point to flatten. The centre of the body will be slightly curved.

cup

This is, perhaps, the simplest model to make, and it is easy to teach to "students" of all ages; it makes a fine children's party fold for the very young. If you intend to drink from the cup, be sure to use material which is glossy, like a foil-backed giftwrap. The predominant colour of the cup, which will be on the outside only, is determined by the colour of the square you begin with face down.

1 Fold the paper in half diagonally.

2 Fold the upper raw edge (single layer only) down to lie along the folded edge created in step 1.

3 Unfold step 2.

4 Fold the right-hand corner over so that the tip meets with the end of the crease made in step 2.

5 Repeat this move on the left side, lining the model up symmetrically, as shown here.

6 Fold the upper corner (single layer only) down tightly over the flaps folded in steps 4–5.

7 Repeat on the reverse side. Open out the model along the upper folded edges to make the cup ready to use.

lily

This is a delightful model, and one of the few flowers that can be presented without a stem, leaves or any other adornment. Its curved petals make it particularly attractive; you can use a pencil to shape them, if you wish.

1 Begin with the Frog base. The open points need to be at the top.

2 Fold all four of the small central triangular flaps back on themselves to face the open points. You will have to swivel the layers of the main flaps around to expose the final two faces, to complete this step.

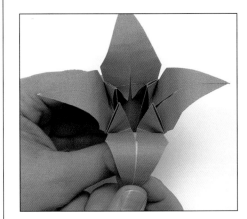

3 Again swivel the layers around, so that the plain smooth faces are uppermost.

4 Beginning at the closed end, narrow the model by folding single layer flaps into the centre. Repeat on all faces.

5 Step 4 completed all the way around.

6 Take two opposite outer "petals", and gently pull apart, allowing the model to open up. It should now be like a four-sided pyramid-shaped cone.

7 Repeat with the two remaining opposite sides of the model, before curling the outer petals. You can use your fingers to do this, or alternatively you can roll the petals over a pencil.

samurai helmet

A large sheet of paper will be required for this model, if you are making one to fit your head. A square from a sheet of standard-size giftwrap should make an impressive model for most small warriors. The helmet appeared in Robert Harbin's first book, *Origami 1*; this design is a simpler version.

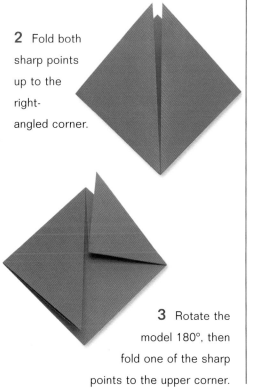

1 Fold the square in half diagonally; the colour then on the outside will be the predominant colour on the finished helmet.

2 Fold both sharp points up to the right-angled corner.

3 Rotate the model 180°, then fold one of the sharp points to the upper corner.

4 Create the horn, by folding the sharp point outwards, as shown. As a guide, try folding the point so that when you have done so the upper edge rests parallel to the horizontal centre crease.

5 Repeat step 4 on the other side. Then fold up a single layer of paper at the bottom, to a point approximately halfway between the top of the helmet and the centre line.

6 Double over the lower folded edge, creating a band across the rim of the helmet.

7 Flatten the model then mountain fold the remaining lower corner so that it meets the top of the helmet. The model is now ready to wear.

kimono

The kimono is a traditional garment worn by both men and women in Japan. Japanese washi paper works wonderfully well for this design, and gives a soft material feel to your finished Kimono. Begin with paper in the proportion of approximately 1:4 (four times as long as wide). A sheet 7 x 28cm/2¾ x 11in will produce a model approximately 8cm/3¼in high: a handy size to mount on a card. Begin with the desired collar colour on top.

1 Begin by pre-creasing along the centre line connecting the shorter sides, and also the thirds-division creases. At one end fold over a thin strip of approximately 5mm/¼in.

2 Turn the paper over, and at the same end fold the corners to the centre line.

3 Use the thirds division creases to concertina the paper, as shown.

4 Take the top two layers of paper at the lower end of the model and fold the side into the centre, making a squash fold of the corner. The squash fold will be off-centre. Repeat on the other side.

5 Lift up the outer edges of the strip folded in step 1, and allow the side section to tuck underneath it.

6 Mountain fold the top edge behind as far as it will go, independently of the central strip.

7 Mountain fold the lower layer of paper up to meet the folded edge created in the previous step. To shape the sleeves, mountain fold the lower corners behind.

crown

Paper hats are extremely popular. Try folding a spread of newspaper cut into a square first, so that you can gauge the size of Crown required, before proceeding to fold one from special paper. Enlarge or reduce the size accordingly.

1 Begin with the Blintz fold. The colour you begin with uppermost is the colour for the inside of the Crown.

2 Turn the paper over. Then fold the lower edge to the horizontal centre crease, at the same time allowing the blintzed flap from beneath to flip around to the front. Press flat.

3 Repeat step 2 on the upper edge.

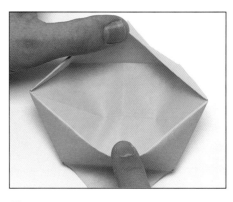

4 Lift up the lower triangular flap, and then fold in both smaller triangled corners to the hinge crease. Repeat with the upper triangular flap.

5 Fold the triangular flaps back down, and flatten the model, trapping the corners folded in step 4.

6 There are two horizontal folded edges running across the centre.

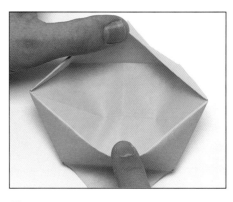

7 Place your fingers inside these edges, and pull apart, opening up a pocket.

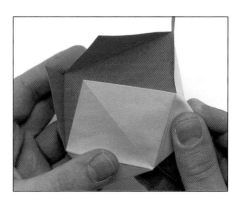

8 Turn the model over at this stage, and pinch in firm creases at the corners, so that the Crown takes on a square shape. Continue shaping the model. Adjust the four points at the top of the Crown to appear even.

shell

Packs of standard origami paper often contain instructions for a simple, traditional model. This design was discovered on the inner sleeve of a small pack of pearlized paper, the shiny surface of which has been used to fold the model featured in the step-folds. Use a square of paper, and begin with the colour you wish to be on the outside of the shell face down.

1 Begin by folding the paper in half diagonally both ways, making these pre-creases. Fold and unfold each time.

2 Blintz fold upper and lower corners to the centre.

3 Turn the paper over, then fold the upper and lower edges inward to meet the horizontal centre crease.

4 Unfold step 3, and turn the paper over.

5 Fold the two side corners inward, the creases connecting the ends of the folds made in step 3.

6 Pinch the paper backward at the horizontal mountain folds created in step 3. Slide the folded edge away from you, until you can bring it down to lie on the horizontal centre crease. Press flat, creasing all the way across the model. This pleats the paper horizontally.

7 Repeat step 6 with the upper edge, then valley fold the model in half, bringing outer corners together.

8 Holding the central section fairly tightly with your left hand, take hold of the outer edge of the model in your right hand. Pull this flap out to the side, so that the pleated area of paper created in step 6 is allowed to stretch.

9 This new crease doesn't reach the outer edge of the shell; it will be necessary to slightly turn the model inside out on itself, curving the surface of the shell. Flatten the paper gently, allowing the shell to keep its curved shape. Repeat on the left-hand side, then on the underside.

10 Shape the final model by adding small mountain folds to the outer edges, to round off the corners.

peace dove

This model, by Alice Gray, has been developed from a traditional idea, and is a symbol of peace and friendship. A clever folding sequence and an economy of moves produce a simple and delightful design, so often the mark of her work. Use a square of fairly thin and crisp paper. After the first fold is made, the inside colour of the paper will not be visible, so it does not really matter what colour this is.

1 Begin with the colour you wish the dove to be face down, and fold the paper in half, corner to corner. Then fold in half again, bringing the two sharp points together, that is, folding the paper into quarters. Arrange as shown, with the main folded edge running horizontally across the top, and the two independent corners pointing downward.

2 Fold the sharp point at the bottom, single layer only, back across to meet the right corner.

3 Repeat step 2 on the reverse face.

4 Fold the new lower corner, single layer only, upward to meet the horizontal edge.

5 Unfold step 4, and inside reverse fold this flap, using the existing crease.

6 Repeat step 5 on the reverse face.

7 Valley fold the closed point at the left downward. The angle is not critical, but you should have a small right-angled triangle projecting outward beyond the lower sloping edge. This will form the head of the dove.

8 Unfold step 7, and inside reverse fold this point on existing creases.

9 Fold the sharp point at the right, single layer only, upward, swinging the flap into position using a natural hinge crease. This will form the nearside wing.

10 Repeat step 9 on the reverse face. Then lift up the triangular section at the right (the tail), making a sharp crease along the edge of the wing section. Raise the point so that it projects upward at right angles to the rest of the model.

11 Symmetrically squash fold the point raised in step 10. This forms a sharp diamond shape.

12 Mountain fold the upper half of this diamond shape behind on the hinge crease, making the model symmetrical once again.

sampan

This traditional design has a very clever final move: the model is turned inside out, locking the layers of paper, and producing a flat-bottomed boat which is very sturdy and right for sailing. Use a fairly large sheet of thin, crisp paper, say A3 (29 x 42cm/11½ x 16½in) cut square, as you will be making lots of folds, one on top of the other, creating quite a thickness of layers.

1 After folding in half diagonally in both directions, to establish starter creases, Blintz fold upper and lower corners to the centre. Whichever colour these blintzed flaps now are, will be the canopy colour on the final model.

2 Unfold step 1, and fold the same corners inward to meet the creases just made.

3 Double over the folded edges once more, using the existing creases.

4 Turn the paper over.

5 Rotate the paper by 90° and repeat steps 1–3 with the remaining corners.

6 Fold the top and bottom horizontal edges to the centre.

7 Fold all four outer corners inward to the horizontal centre line.

8 On the right-hand end, double over the folded edges created in step 7, narrowing them to a point.

9 Repeat step 8 on the left point. These flaps will slightly overlap the folds made in step 8.

10 Fold the outer corners top and bottom into the centre. The layers will be thick, so fold carefully and accurately.

11 There are two folded edges that meet along the centre line. Place your fingers underneath these edges, and open the model out, gripping these flaps and the triangular sections, created in step 10, between fingers and thumbs.

12 Turn the model over, but keep holding it as in step 11. Your thumbs should now be over the underside of the hull, just short of one canopy section.

13 In one movement, push down with your thumbs, while using your fingers to pull the sides of the boat from underneath into a position on top, so that the model turns inside out.

14 Repeat step 13 at the other end of the boat. Pinch-crease and shape the hull, and the canopies, and carefully round the canopies into a gentle curve.

masu box

This traditional box has a lid and compartment divider, which can be made using the reverse side of the paper to give a contrasting colour. The Masu Box can be used to contain all kinds of things from paper clips to jewellery. This folding method is as taught by David Brill. Paulo Bascetta designed the compartment divider. You will need three squares of fairly sturdy paper, of equal size.

1 To make the box, fold two opposite sides of the first square in half to meet each other, to determine the centre crease. The colour on the inside will be the colour of the completed box.

2 Open out the paper. Rotate it around so that the crease made in step 1 is vertical to you, then fold it in half again, using the remaining edges. Rotate the paper 180° so that the crease made in step 2 now becomes the upper edge.

3 Fold each of the lower corners upward (single layer only), so that the lower edges meet with the vertical centre crease, while the outer edges meet with the upper folded edge. Turn over and repeat on the reverse face.

4 Open out the main crease made in step 2, then lay the paper back on your folding surface with the blintzed flaps on top, and the paper arranged as a square, with horizontals and verticals.

5 Fold the lower edge inward to meet with the centre of the paper. Make a really sharp crease all the way across the paper.

6 Unfold step 5. Make sure that the inner blintzed corner doesn't unfold out with the rest of the paper.

7 Rotate the paper around, repeating step 5 on the remaining three sides of the square, on each occasion folding and unfolding the paper. The photograph shows the crease pattern at this stage.

8 Completely open out the blintzed corners at left and right.

9 Refold the upper and lower folded edges back to the centre on creases made in step 5.

10 Take hold of each end of the model as shown, your thumbs should rest on top of the paper, the outer edges of your index fingers beneath. If you look at each end of the model, there are two vertical creases coming down through the paper, creating a rectangular area in-between; your thumbs should be placed in-between these two creases, so that they are outside of the short diagonal folds made earlier.

11 Lift up the two ends of the paper you are holding, allowing the inner portion of the model to become a three-dimensional box form. The two horizontal borders from step 9 will become two sides of the box, and the edges just between your thumbs will become the remaining two sides.

12 When you release your hold, there will be two large flaps projecting outward at the sides. Turn the box around so that you are looking at the outside of the flaps, then mountain fold them inward over the edges of the box.

13
Box completed.
Now for the lid and the divider. ▶

14 To make the lid, begin with step 4 of the box.

15 Repeat step 5, only this time do not bring the lower edge to the centre of the paper, but stop about 3mm/⅛in short, leaving the tip of the blintzed flap still in view. Repeat on the opposite edge.

16 To check whether the lid will be a nice snug fit, raise the folded edges so that they project upwards at right angles to the base. Insert the completed Box in-between the two crease lines. The lid should fit comfortably. Repeat this step in the other direction.

17 Finish the lid off in exactly the same way as you made the box.

18 Fit the completed lid to the box.

19 If you wish to have the divider the reverse colour of the paper to the box and lid, begin with the reverse colour on top. Crease along both diagonals, folding and unfolding each time.

20 Turn the paper over, and then fold in half side to side in both directions, again folding and unfolding each time.

21 Add thirds-division creases horizontally.

22 Rotate the paper. Add thirds-division creases in the other direction by folding the lower edge to meet with the intersection of the diagonal creases and the first set of thirds-division creases.

23 Unfold. The crease pattern completed.

24 Fold all four corners inward to touch the outer corners of the central square.

25 Fold the outer raw edges inward.

26 Collapse into a Waterbomb base, with all the flaps on the outside.

27 Fold the top point of the Waterbomb base down to the lower edge.

28 Take hold of the lower edge of the model along with the small triangle folded in step 27, and open out, separating the two outer sections. The central area of the paper will not lie flat.

BELOW The completed Divider will sit in the Box.

29 There is a crease running horizontally across the paper. Mountain fold the model in half using this crease. If you place the model back on the folding surface and press down firmly, the shape of the divider will become apparent.

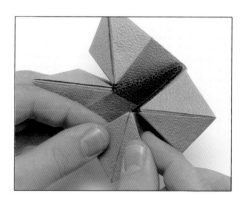

30 Turn the model over, and, using fingers and thumbs, pinch-crease around all the base folds of the model, to define the creases already made.

nun

This model, by Kunihiko Kasahara, makes fine use of the two colours on reverse sides of the paper. Use a sheet of fairly crisp paper, with the face and hands colour on top to begin with.

2 Fold the lower corner up to a point a short way down from the top, and then fold this corner back down toward you, again by a small amount. These folds aren't particularly critical, so you may wish to experiment.

3 Fold the sloping left-hand edge inward over the edge of the flap folded up in step 2.

1 Begin by folding the paper in half, corner to corner, to pre-crease one diagonal. Open out, and arrange the paper so that this crease is now vertical.

4 Repeat step 3 with the upper right-hand edge.

5 Pull out the hidden corner at the overlap of the flaps folded in steps 3–4.

6 Squash this corner to a point. Also fold the outer corners of the long border strips inward, to form the hands.

7 Mountain fold the model in half using the vertical centre crease.

8 Fold the lower flap at the right (single layer only) upward and across to the left, bringing the hand into position.

9 Shape the nun's back by valley folding the outer right corner across, as shown.

10 After repeating steps 8–9 on the reverse face, open up the vertical centre fold made in step 7 slightly, allowing the model to stand.

butterfly

This subject is one of the most popular to fold in origami, and there is a Japanese master by the name of Akira Yoshizawa who has folded numerous different species with many variations. For this simple design by Paul Jackson, use a square of fairly thin, crisp paper. Why not try and invent your own butterfly model, perhaps using some of the techniques and ideas used in this book?

3 Valley fold the lower extreme corners by a small amount, as shown.

1 Begin with a Waterbomb base. Rotate upside down from its best-known position.

4 Unfold step 3.

2 Fold the lower corner up to the top edge.

5 Carefully refold step 3, but folding the upper single layer of paper only this time. For this you will need to slightly open out the "pocket" along the edge of the triangular flap folded in step 2.

6 Step 5 complete.

7 Fold both uppermost flaps of the Waterbomb base downward close to the vertical centre line. These are the hind wings.

8 Mountain fold the model in half, bringing the two sets of wings together. The illustration shows this fold arranged to lie along the top horizontally, and the larger front wings are to the right.

9 Taking the single layer only, fold the nearest front wing to you upward, on a crease that is at a slight angle to the upper edge. Repeat on the reverse face; there will be a very acute V shape formed by the wing creases, and the body will now form a central angled ridge (see the final photograph).

10 Allow the butterfly's wings to open naturally and display as shown.

swan

This is a simple variation on classic swan designs; however, the swivel move to define the neck and head requires practice. Begin with a square of fairly thin, crisp paper.

1 Begin with a Fish base, arranged as shown.

2 Fold the point at the left (both thicknesses) over to the right corner.

3 Mountain fold the model in half along the horizontal centre crease.

4 Hold the lower portion of the body between finger and thumb of one hand, whilst holding the neck point with finger and thumb of the other hand. Begin sliding the sharp point up and away from the body, flattening the model into a new position.

5 Step 4 half completed.

6 The swivel. Fold the rear edge of the neck (one layer only) forward, narrowing the neck. At the same time, push up on the lower corner, bringing it into a new position, which makes the body thinner. There isn't an exact location for this crease; you will discover by a little trial and error how best to form the body and neck. The crease does not meet the tip of the neck at the point, but a little way down the rear edge. Flatten the model.

7 Repeat step 6 on the reverse face.

8 Step 7 completed.

9 Form an outside reverse fold close to the tip, to create the head.

10 Separate the tips of the beak and allow the body to open out slightly to complete the swan.

scottie dog

This simple model uses a very clever folding sequence, whereby a flap is pulled out, forming the Scottie's head. Models like this do not have any detail, yet they produce impressive results of simplicity and elegance. This model was designed by Robert Neale. Begin with a 12cm/4½in square of crisp paper.

1 Begin by creasing in both diagonals of the square, folding and unfolding each time. With predominant colour underneath, Blintz fold all the corners to the centre.

2 Fold the right blintzed flap outwards, so that one-third of the flap projects outward beyond the right-hand edge. Mountain fold the tip of the left blintzed flap underneath, again by approximately a third of itself.

3 Valley fold the model in half using the horizontal centre crease, folding the upper edge down to meet the lower edge.

4 Fold the lower left-hand corner, single layer only, upward, on a crease which connects the upper left corner and the lower right corner, allowing the inner blintzed flap to lie released to the front.

5 Repeat step 4 on the reverse face, matching up the two flaps once folded.

6 With your index finger, pull out the extra paper hidden inside the front of the head.

buttonhole flower

Combining the creative talents of Alice Gray and
Paul Jackson, this simple flower is a real joy.
Fold using two squares of paper of
identical size, preferably of duo paper.
A 7–8cm/2¾–3¼in square piece
of paper is an ideal size for
a buttonhole.

1 Make the leaf by folding a Kite base
with the predominant colour underneath.
Rotate to the position shown.

2 Fold the two shorter sloping edges
into the centre line.

3 Rotate the paper 180°, then valley
fold the model in half along the
centre crease.

▶

4 Turn 90° clockwise. Fold the left-hand sloping edge (single layer only) upward to lie on the horizontal folded edge.

5 Repeat step 4 on the reverse. Then open out the wider end of the leaf, pinch-folding the upper section tightly over the diagonal fold line crossing the model. Press down firmly, so that the leaf remains three-dimensional.

6 Step 5 seen from the reverse side. The completed leaf.

7 To make the flower, begin by folding a Waterbomb base, the outer colour will be the outer colour of the final flower.

8 Fold the model in half, bringing all the sharp points together.

9 Fold the closed point inward on a crease that also meets the right-angled corner. This should produce an acutely pointed triangular section.

10 Take hold of the two independent sharp points at the rear of the model, and wrap them around to the front, so that the triangular section formed in step 9 now lies between two lots of two flaps.

11 Step 10 completed.

12 Holding the small triangular point of the section formed in step 9 in one hand, allow the four large flaps to fan out, so that there is one pointing in all four N, S, E, W directions.

13 Allowing each of the larger points to open out slightly, use the thumb of your free hand to pinch-fold the area of paper at the base of each flap in turn. At the same time, push down on the outer crease and softly flatten the paper, so that each petal remains open.

14 The completed flower.

15 Insert the small triangular "stem" of the flower into the pocket of the leaf, which is formed by the diagonal edge cutting across the outer face of the model. (A little glue may help to hold the flower in place.)

ABOVE The completed Buttonhole Flower.

rooster

It is always a useful exercise to practise certain basic techniques. Here, a few simple inside and outside reverse folds are used to form a stylized yet recognizable creation, designed by Florence Temko. You will find that the angles of these reverse folds are often left up to you, and the final model will depend upon such choices. Begin with a square of fairly sturdy paper.

1 Begin with a Fish base, arranged as shown.

2 Open out the two layers of paper at the sharper point, swinging the rear flap behind and across to the left.

3 Mountain fold the paper in half along the horizontal centre crease, folding the lower half behind.

4 Make a preparatory valley fold with the right-hand point, bringing it into a position lying along the vertical centre line.

5 Inside reverse fold this point.

6 Repeat step 5 with the left point; this time it is difficult to pre-fold, because you risk creasing the two small triangular fins at the side. Therefore, make this fold independent of the side flaps.

7 Inside reverse fold both points to the positions shown. The right point (the head) can rest pointing slightly higher than the one on the left (the tail), if you like.

8 Outside reverse fold the tail. Inside reverse fold the head twice, firstly taking the point across to the left, inside the head section.

9 Then bring the point back out again, forming the head and beak.

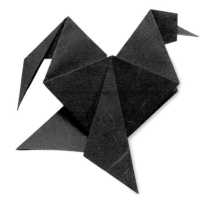

10 On the side facing you, fold the small fin down at a desired angle, to form a leg.

11 Form the foot by folding the tip of this flap back up again. When the folds are completed this will finally be brought into a position at right angles with the body, enabling the model to stand freely.

12 Repeat steps 10–11 on the reverse face to complete the Rooster.

human figure

Alfred Bestall, illustrator for Rupert Bear, was a keen exponent of origami, and introduced paperfolding into the stories about this little bear and all his friends from Nutwood. Take four sheets of paper, the first two squares of the same size. For the third sheet of paper (the head), trim a square of the same size in half, then fold the paper into thirds-division creases, with creases parallel to the short sides. Trim off one-third of this 2 : 1 rectangle. Use the larger of these pieces of paper to make the head, the smaller remaining piece of paper to make the hat.

1 Using paper the same colour on each side, fold and unfold the first square in half, corner to corner, to determine the two diagonal creases. Then Blintz fold the four corners to the centre.

2 Turn the paper over. Arrange the paper so that it appears as a diamond shape, then fold upper and lower corners to the centre.

3 Turn the paper over. Keeping the corners out to the left and right, fold the two lower edges upward to lie on the vertical centre line. The outer corners come to meet with the ends of the upper horizontal edge.

4 Repeat step 3 at the top of the model, bringing the upper edges down to lie along the vertical centre line. The illustration shows the right side completed.

5 At the right side, slide out the hidden extra paper, underneath the overlap of flaps folded in steps 3–4.

6 Squeeze the paper to a point, and flatten downwards towards you. Repeat steps 4–6 on the left side of the model. Steps 4–6 completed.

7 Turn the model over. At top and bottom, there are two diamond shapes, with a vertical slit pocket. On the bottom diamond, push outward on the innermost corner, allowing the paper to hollow outward, and then squash flat into a rectangle. Repeat step 7 at the top of the model.

 8 Step 7 completed. This forms the upper body and arms.

9 For the lower body and legs, take the remaining square of paper and follow steps 1–8, making another unit identical to the upper body and arms. Fold the unit in half so that the two rectangular-shaped squash folds meet.

10 Connect the two sections by inserting the rectangular shape at the upper end of the legs into the rectangular shape at the lower end of the body.

11 With the larger of the two remaining rectangular sheets of paper, fold the paper in half, bringing the two shorter sides together. Fold in half again (into quarters), and unfold, establishing the vertical centre crease. Fold the two upper folded corners down to lie along the vertical centre line.

12 Fold the lower edge, single layer only, upward so that it comes to rest along the lower edges of the triangular flaps. Double this strip over, then repeat on the reverse face.

13 Slide the head onto the rectangle at the upper end of the body.

14 Lock into place by mountain folding the outer corners of the head behind. Widen the creases slightly at the upper end to shape the face.

15 Fold a hat from the remaining rectangle of paper, following steps 11–12. Slide the hat on to the head. Fix it with a little glue, if you wish.

goldfish

Designed by Japanese folder Masamichi Noma, this creation features a wonderfully clever lock for the tail, and is a model with real character. Begin with a square of paper preferably textured on the predominant-coloured side. The colour you begin with face up provides the reverse colour for the eye.

1 Fold and unfold the paper in half, bottom to top, to determine the horizontal centre crease. Then fold upper and lower edges to the centre line. Fold both the outer corners at the left inward to lie along the horizontal centre line.

2 Unfold these corners, then inside reverse fold them.

3 Step 2 completed.

4 At the right side of the model, fold both outer corners inward to lie along the horizontal centre line.

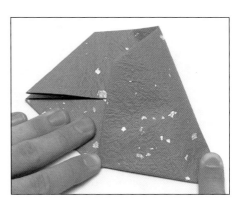

5 Fold the right corner across to the left, until it meets the obtuse angle along the lower left edge. Pinch-crease close to the lower edge only. This will mark a point along the lower edge by which to make a later fold.

6 Repeat step 5, folding and unfolding the right point to the obtuse angle along the upper edge. This time, pinch-crease a mark along the upper edge.

7 Fold the left-hand point across to the right, so that the obtuse outer angles meet with the two pinch-marks made in steps 5–6. Make a vertical valley crease down the paper.

8 Fold this point back out to the left upon itself, making a pleat in the model. The obtuse outer angles of the flap you are folding will rest upon the extreme right angles of the portion of paper beneath.

9 Swing both loose points at the left (single layer only) across to the right on their natural hinge creases. Unfold step 4 at the right-hand end of the model.

10 Fold each of the loose points outward to the outer edges of the model, as far as they will comfortably go.

11 Raise each of the points on the hinge crease this creates, and squash fold each one, making half Preliminary bases.

12 Step 11 completed.

13 Fold the inner corners of the squashed preliminary shapes outwards as far as they will comfortably go, to reveal the eye colour.

14 Shape the top left, top right, and bottom right corners of the upper eye with tiny mountain folds. Repeat in mirror image with the lower eye.

15 Fold the left point across to the right so that it meets the inner corners of the eyes.

▶

16 Fold this point back outward to the left, so that approximately one-third of its length now projects beyond the folded edge beneath it.

17 Mountain fold the tip of this point behind, tightly over the folded edge beneath it.

18 Mountain fold the model in half along the horizontal crease line, folding the top portion down behind, so that the eyes are on the outside.

19 Fold all the layers at the short, vertical right-hand edge down on a diagonal crease, so that they lie along the lower edge. Crease firmly.

20 Unfold step 19. Fold the upper right corner downward once more, this time on a crease that connects a point just to the side of the eye, with the lower right corner. Again fold all the layers as one.

21 Unfold step 20, then inside reverse fold this flap on existing creases.

22 Open out the tail section, and fold up the two loose inside corners only, using the creases made in step 19.

23 Step 22 completed.

24 Mountain fold the tip of the tail, upper layer only, to a point approximately halfway across the entire flap (where the vertical crease runs through the tail fins).

25 Repeat for the other tail tip. This will be a valley fold as you look.

26 Unfold the fold made in step 24. Also unfold the near-side flap completely (steps 21–22).

27 Refold the near-side tail flap behind (step 24) then refold steps 21–22 on the near-side layer of paper. (This changes the sequence in which these last steps are performed.)

28 Step 27 in progress. Note the little pleated tuck in the outer front layer of the tail section.

29 The triangular section of paper folded inwards in step 25 has a folded edge cutting across it, which forms a very narrow pocket. As you close and flatten the model, insert the little tuck created in step 28 into this pocket. It will slide down into place.

BELOW The completed Goldfish.

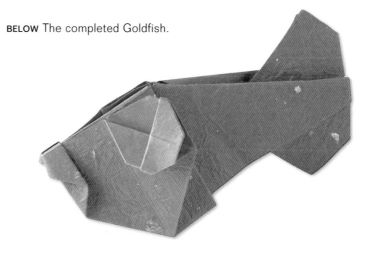

rabbit

Created by Edwin Corrie, this is a classic among many animal folds that he has designed. What is particularly clever is the use of duo paper, with white folded on the inside, to emerge later as the fluffy tail. The reverse side of the paper can often produce fine details, such as on animals and faces. A square of fairly thin paper works best for this model.

1 With the white side of the paper on top, and having first pre-creased horizontally to find the centre line, fold opposite edges in to the middle.

2 Turn the paper over, and fold the two corners on the right inward to the centre crease.

3 Rotate the model through 90° and turn back over to the original side. Fold the point upward, on a crease that connects the two lower angles of step 2. This crease runs along the edges of the flaps folded in step 2.

4 Holding one half of the triangle with one hand, take hold of the top corner point at the other side, and slide it outward to the side. Allow the hidden paper to slide out also, until eventually you will be able to flatten it to a point.

5 Step 4 completed on one side.

6 Repeat step 4 on the remaining side.

7 Fold the lower edge up, folding the lower portion in half.

8 Unfold step 7, then make a 45° crease with each flap, bringing the lower edge to lie along the vertical centre crease, and the sharp points to align with the vertical outer edges.

9 Open out step 8.

10 Taking hold of each of the sharp points, manoeuvre them back into the position shown in step 8, whilst collapsing the middle section as shown. The sharp points are folded in half as this all happens, and the inner paper collapses and swings into position. Flatten the model.

11 Step 10 completed.

12 Mountain fold the tip of the lower point underneath. This will form the nose; the amount you fold isn't critical. ▶

13 Mountain fold the large section of paper behind, as far as it will comfortably go. The crease runs along the edge of the head section.

14 Mountain fold the model in half along the vertical centre crease, and arrange as shown.

15 Holding the head with one hand, take hold of the lower portion of the paper with the other, and pull it through, turning it inside out on itself, and making an inside reverse fold. The crease begins where the index finger of the left hand is located, that is just below the base of the ear.

16 Flatten the model.

17 To narrow the ears using swivel folds, look at the small triangle at the base of the ear. Open out slightly, then push forward on the spine crease, swivelling the ear into the position shown.

18 Step 17 completed on one ear.

19 Along the rear edge of the head there are two folded edges running together, which give a pocket. Open out slightly, and tuck the tiny triangle created by the swivel fold in step 17 into this pocket. Flatten the model, then repeat steps 17–19 for the other ear.

20 At the tail, mountain fold the outer layer only inside. Repeat on the reverse. This exposes the white for the tail colour. Also shape the head, with mountain folds, taking the rear edges under.

21 Make two inside reverse folds to finish the tail; the first takes the tail inside the model, on a crease which runs along the edges of the folds made in step 20.

22 The second fold brings the tail out and back into view, as shown.

23 Steps 21 and 22 completed.

24 Mountain fold the upper layer of the lower portion of the paper inside, at an angle that will eventually allow the model to stand without falling over.

25 Repeat step 24 on the reverse, then open out the model slightly so the Rabbit sits up happily, as shown.

tulip and vase

Models that have been independently designed can often be put together to wonderful effect. Such as this combination of models: the Vase, created by the late Toshie Takahama; the Stem and Tulip designed by Kunihiko Kasahara. For the Vase and the Stem, use squares of equal size. For the Tulip, use a square a quarter of the size of the two other squares. Use fairly stiff paper.

1 To make the vase begin with a Preliminary base, predominant colour outside, and with the open flaps at the top.

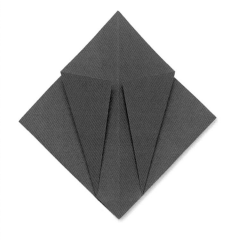

2 Fold the side corners, one layer only each side, in towards the centre line. The creases make the angle of these folds taper in narrower at the bottom than at the top.

3 Repeat on the reverse face.

4 Fold the upper left-hand corner, one layer only, down to meet with the vertical centre line.

5 Allowing the flap folded in step 4 to open up slightly, now fold the main central flap at the top down.

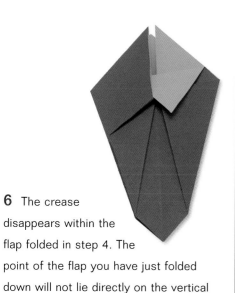

6 The crease disappears within the flap folded in step 4. The point of the flap you have just folded down will not lie directly on the vertical centre crease but will rest instead slightly to the right.

7 Fold over one of the main flaps from the right across to the left, using the vertical centre crease as a hinge.

8 Repeat step 4 on the next upper left-hand flap. Fold down the main upper flap, as in step 5.

9 Turn the model over, and repeat step 8 on the upper left-hand flap.

10 Once again, fold the main flap from right over to the left, using the vertical centre crease.

11 Repeat step 4 on the remaining upper left-hand corner.

▶

12 On the right-hand side of the model, you are now back where you began. Partially unhook the folded flap from behind.

13 Pull the final raw corner down into position.

14 Refold, and adjust all the folds within each layer, as shown.

15 Flatten the model. Fold the lower corner upward, on a crease that connects the outer extreme corners. Crease firmly and unfold.

16 Open out the vase, hollowing and shaping with your fingers.

17 To help the model to stand, use your finger and thumb to pinch-fold all four creases around the base.

18 The completed Vase.

19 To make the stem begin with a Kite base, with dark green the predominant colour underneath.

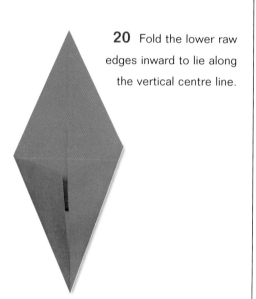

20 Fold the lower raw edges inward to lie along the vertical centre line.

21 At the other end of the model, narrow the stem further by folding the outer sloping edges to the centre line.

22 Valley fold the model in half, bringing the wider flap up to rest on the sharper point.

23 Mountain fold the model in half along the vertical centre crease, such that the sharper point will be on the inside.

24 Holding the outer section (the leaf) with one hand, and the sharper point (the stem) in the other, slide the stem outwards, and flatten the model so that the stem adopts a new position.

25 The completed Stem.

26 Place the stem into the vase.

▶

27 To make the tulip begin with a Preliminary base, predominant colour outside, and with the open flaps at the top.

28 Fold in the flaps at the side to lie along the centre crease. Note: the points land a short way down from the centre of the model, so that the bud is wider at the base than it is at the top.

29 Unfold step 28. Fold in the upper edges to lie along the creases made in step 28.

30 Refold on the creases made in step 28, doubling the flaps over.

31 Repeat steps 28–30 on the reverse face.

32 With scissors, snip off a tiny bit of the closed point; when the tulip is opened out this will produce a square-shaped hole, used to mount the flower on the stem. Only cut a very small piece away, for example 3mm (⅛in) for a tulip made from a 10.5cm (4⅛in) square.

33 Carefully open out the tulip, hollowing out at the opening, and shaping with your fingers.

ABOVE The completed tulip and vase.

34 Allowing the tulip to keep its shape, carefully lower the flower on to the stem. Push down gently until the tulip has gripped the stem. It should remain upright once you have released your hand.

elephant

There is a group of young Japanese
enthusiasts who call themselves The
Tanteidan, and they tend to specialize
in fairly complex folds, often with
spectacular results. This elephant,
though not particularly difficult
to make, was designed by group
member Nobuyoshi Enomoto.
Sturdy grey paper works best, and a fairly large sheet is
recommended, say a 21cm/8¼in square, for your first attempt.

1 Begin with the Fish
base, with the predominant colour for the model on the outside.

2 Pull apart the two sharp points at the right side, opening the
model out so that you can spread the base flat as a diamond
shape. The two small triangular flaps should point to the left as
you look at the model.

3 Mountain fold the lower half of the model behind, using the
horizontal centre crease.

4 Valley fold the right point down at 45° to
the rest of the model, so that the upper edge
comes to rest along the hinge crease of the
small triangular flap at the side.

5 Keeping the sloping outer right-hand
edge in line with itself, fold this point
back upwards and across, taking the tip a
little further than the corner now lying
beneath. This forms the hind legs, rump
and tail.

6 Fold the excess paper projecting beyond the far right corner down once more, to suggest the tail.

7 Opening out steps 4–6, continue by now recreating these steps with outside reverse folds.

8 Step 7 completed.

9 Swing the small triangular side flaps, front and back, across to the right, using the natural hinge creases.

10 Valley fold the left corner, the remaining large point, upward, as far as it will comfortably go, so that the corner beneath lies approximately halfway across this point.

11 The model, temporarily turned over, shows the location of the crease made in step 10.

▶

12 Unfold step 10.

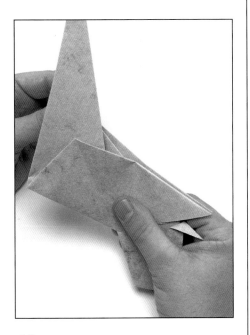

13 Now inside reverse fold this flap using existing creases.

14 Valley fold the large point back downward, on a crease that runs in line with the horizontal upper edge.

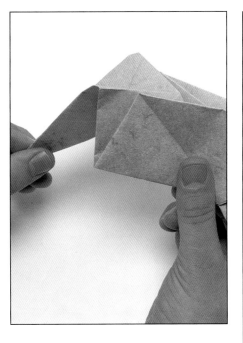

15 Unfold step 14, and inside reverse fold the point down on existing creases.

16 Step 15 complotod.

17 Locate the lower left corner close to the large point. Fold this upward to lie along the upper edge. Repeat on the reverse face.

18 Unfold step 17, and inside reverse fold this corner into the model. You will need to push the paper in, and keep pushing until it will not go any further. A new mountain fold will form which runs all the way to the corner of what will be a newly created small triangular flap on the outside.

19 Step 18 completed. This forms the ear.

20 Fold down the triangular flap pointing to the right, so that the upper edge swivels to lie along the edge of the mountain fold created by the inside reverse fold in step 18. This will be the front leg.

21 Valley fold the tip of the flap folded in step 20 upward.

22 Unfold step 21. The small triangle created in step 21 now needs to be tucked away inside the model. For this, you will need to open out the front leg section, so that the point can be folded up inside on the pre-crease.

23 Step 22 completed.

24 Swing the ear across to the right on the natural hinge crease.

25 Repeat steps 17–24 on the reverse face.

26 Fold the large flap at the left (the head) down, carefully folding the single layer only, thus opening the head out flat. Mountain fold down the remaining half of the head section. Care needs to be taken not to force the paper too hard against the spine crease of the head, which may cause the paper to crease messily, or even tear.

27 Valley fold the head point down at a certain angle, to create the fold required for the trunk.

28 Unfold step 27.

29 Inside reverse fold the trunk.

▶

30 Narrow the trunk by making a valley fold that takes the front edge to the rear edge. The crease should not come all the way down to the end of the trunk. Repeat on the reverse face.

31 Make two to three more reverse folds at certain angles, to complete the folding of the trunk.

32 Valley fold the tip of the ear forward.

33 Open out the ear slightly, in order to inside reverse fold this small triangular flap into the model. Repeat on the other ear.

34 Step 33 completed.

35 Valley fold the hind legs upward, so that the crease you make runs in line with the lower edge of the front legs.

36 Unfold step 35. Turn the model upside down, and carefully open out the hind leg section. This will allow you, as with the front legs, to roll the portion of paper at the end of the hind legs inside the model on the crease made in step 35.

38 The outer rear corner of the hind legs needs to be pushed in slightly (a contrived inside reverse fold, as the layers are really too thick by now to first make a preparatory valley fold).

37 Step 36 in progress.

39 Step 38 in progress.

40 Open out the front and hind legs slightly, to help the model stand freely.

peacock

This is, perhaps, one of the more complex models in this book. For your first attempt you will need to fold extremely carefully, preferably using a large 2:1 rectangle of crisp paper. The model, a true classic, and one that looks wonderful folded from a banknote, was designed by the late Adolfo Cerceda. Unlike the majority of models in the book, a lot is left to your own initiative. Understanding the folding techniques, and your folding expertise, will affect the success of the final result. Do not attempt this model until you are totally confident with all the basic techniques and procedures.

1 Begin with the side you wish to be the predominant colour face down. Have the paper arranged with the longest sides horizontal, then fold in half in both directions, folding and unfolding each time, to establish the central creases.

2 Fold the two outer corners at the left-hand end to the horizontal centre line.

3 Unfold, then fold a Waterbomb base at the same end of the paper.

4 Raise the sharp point of the Waterbomb base furthest away from you, so that it projects upward at right angles to the rest of the model.

5 Squash fold this point symmetrically.

6 Fold this squashed section in half, top to bottom, using the natural hinge crease that goes through its centre.

7 Fold the short, sloping edge of this section back upward to the horizontal fold line, so that the reverse colour disappears.

8 Swing the entire squashed section upward on the hinge crease, then repeat step 7 on the reverse face.

9 Unfold back to step 5. Note the creases you have made.

10 Now petal fold the paper: take hold of the inner point of this squashed section, and fold it outward to the left, so that it meets with the extreme left corner. You will need to make this crease, although, as a guide, you actually connect the ends of the two creases made in steps 7–8.

11 The creases made in steps 7–8 now come into play, as the sides squash inward, and line up along the horizontal centre crease. Flatten the model.

12 Fold the point created by the petal fold back across to the right on the natural hinge crease.

▶

13 Fold the squashed section in half away from you, bottom to top.

14 Repeat steps 4–13 on the lower half of the model.

15 Take hold of each of the sharp points (the legs), and separate them apart, pulling open gently as shown.

16 Mountain fold the small central triangle up inside the model.

17 Now allow the paper to collapse back again. Flatten the model.

18 Valley fold each of the sharp points outward, making preparatory creases for the following step.

19 Inside reverse fold both sharp points into the position shown.

20 Fold the lower single layer of each leg upwards, opening out to a kite shape.

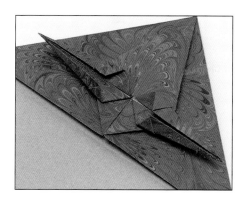

21 Narrow each leg by valley folding the outer edges to the centre crease.

22 Refold the legs back in half, top to bottom.

23 Fold the remaining upper sloping edges of the Waterbomb base to the vertical centre line, making sure they tuck underneath the leg sections. You will need to lift each leg flap up slightly to allow this to be done.

24 Pinch in a horizontal mountain crease across the model, cutting through the point where the corners of the flaps folded in step 23 meet. You will need to lift the paper up off your folding surface to do this. Unfold.

25 Step 24 completed. This is the first tail fold.

26 Now pinch in another crease by taking hold of the mountain fold from step 24, and sliding it away from you, until it lands upon the point at the base of the leg sections. Press down, making another horizontal crease.

27 Allow step 26 to unfold.

28 Fold up the lower edge to meet the crease made in step 26.

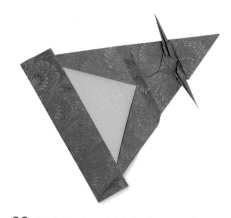

29 Unfold, then fold the lower edge to meet the crease made in step 28. Here we are creating a concertina effect: pleating the paper this way and that, to form the tail. We do this by adding a series of valley and mountain folds to the lower end of the model.

30 Change the crease made in step 26 from a valley to a mountain fold, then use the same process of division to drag this crease down to the line made in step 28. Crease again.

▶

31 Add further divisions until you have at least eight equal pleats in the paper, as shown.

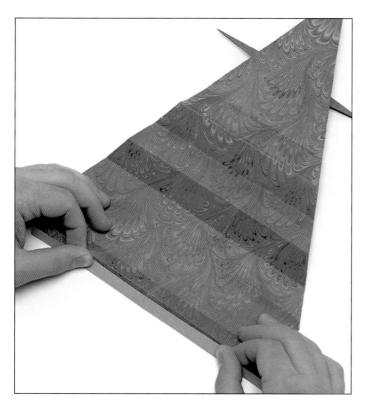

32 Turn the paper over, then add additional horizontal crease lines in between all the creases already made, thus enabling you to pleat the paper into 16th divisions.

33 Start gathering all the pleats. The first fold on the predominantly patterned side shown here is a valley fold.

34 The pleats gathered.

35 With the predominantly coloured side on top, unfold just the final pleat at the lower edge.

36 Turn the model over.

37 Fold the left upper sloping edge of the body section down to lie along the natural horizontal line. Unfold and repeat in the other direction. The next stage will make a rabbit ear out of the whole of the upper section of the body.

38 Holding the pleated tail section down, squeeze the upper section to a point using the two creases made in step 37.

39 At the same time, mountain fold the tail section in half, bringing both ends of the pleated area together.

▶

40 Turn the model over, and notice where the two edges of the unfolded lower edge from step 35 now meet. To join these without the aid of glue, fold the outer corners of these long strips together as one.

41 Double over the whole section, and tuck in-between neighbouring pleats. Squeeze the whole tail section together firmly, to ensure that the lock holds.

42 Outside reverse fold the upper body.

43 Step 42 completed.

44 Fold the rear edge of the neck section forward, creating a swivel and a squash fold simultaneously, to shape the neck and chest.

45 Add an outside reverse fold to create the head, and further reverse folds to suggest a beak.

46 Inside reverse fold the legs backwards.

47 Inside reverse fold the leg back into a forward position, developing the position of the upper and lower leg.

48 Add reverse folds for the feet.

49 The completed Peacock. The tail can rest on your folding surface.

50 Or you can push the tail up from behind the Peacock, so that the tail feathers display.

index